I HOPE IT FLOATS!

Margaret Fetty

Contents

Rigby
A Harcourt Achieve Imprint

www.Rigby.com
1-800-531-5015

A WET AND WACKY RACE

It's a lovely day down by the river. White, puffy clouds drift overhead, while a variety of boats float upon the water. Groups of people sit or stand along the bank to watch the colorful boats race past. On the dock, judges in blue T-shirts hold clipboards and stopwatches as they look out at the boats.

A man in a red canoe speeds quickly across the river's smooth surface. He plunges his paddle into the dark water—first to one side of the boat and then the other. The crowd yells encouragingly as the man increases his speed with each stroke. They break into a loud cheer as he glides past the finish line to take first place!

Judges watch the boats as the captains prepare to start the race.

A red canoe finishes the race first.

A gray canoe and a yellow submarine follow in the distance. The people in both boats paddle furiously, trying to be the team that takes second place. A huge shark can be seen floating even farther down the river. It rocks from side to side, in danger of tipping over. The crowd gives another cheer as the big shark regains its balance and finally makes its way to the finish line.

Wait a minute! What was that last boat—a big *shark*? What is a shark doing in a boat race?

Crowds can expect some amazing sights.

Welcome to the world of cardboard boat racing! All around the country, people get together in basements, garages, and back yards to build boats out of cardboard. But why would someone build a boat out of cardboard? Wouldn't cardboard get soggy and mushy in the water? Wouldn't a cardboard boat leak, or even sink, if people tried to ride in it? Believe it or not, some cardboard boats work very well!

People use their creativity when they design cardboard boats!

A lot of effort went into the building of this frog boat.

People build and race cardboard boats for many different reasons. They do it mostly just for fun. They see the races as a chance to show off their creativity and sense of humor. For instance, some people try to make their boats look like dragons or school buses. Other people enjoy the challenge of solving the difficult problem of making a boat out of cardboard that actually floats. One thing, however, is almost certain—everyone who takes part in a cardboard boat race has a great time.

AN ARTISTIC BEGINNING

Would it surprise you to learn that the person who came up with the idea for the first cardboard boat race was a teacher? It's true! In the 1970s, an art teacher at Southern Illinois University decided to give his students a special project. He challenged them to build boats out of **corrugated** cardboard, the material used to make big, sturdy boxes for things like televisions and washing machines. Students would be graded on three points: each cardboard boat had to float with a person sitting inside it; passengers had to **propel,** or move, their boats on the water using only the power of their own hands or feet; finally, since it was an art class, students had to decorate their boats in a creative way. The students would have several weeks to complete their boats.

Corrugated cardboard

A college student
gets ready to build
a cardboard boat.

How does someone build a boat out of cardboard? At first it seemed like an impossible thing to do. But students soon found corrugated cardboard to be a very strong material. It is made of a wavy piece of thick paper glued between two more flat pieces of thick paper. The three layers together make the cardboard stiff and strong, but still lightweight. Cardboard can be easily bent and cut to make almost any shape. Students found that gluing two or three layers of cardboard together could make the bottom or sides of a boat even stiffer and stronger.

A student works with corrugated cardboard.

A lot of tape and glue are used in a cardboard boat.

The students were allowed to use a few other materials to finish their boats. They used glue to stick pieces of the boat together. Tape was used to cover the cut edges of the cardboard. Caulk, a sticky, gooey, glue-like material, sealed the places where different pieces of cardboard came together so water wouldn't leak into the boat. As a finishing touch, students also used paint to decorate their boats with color, interesting designs, or funny words, so the boats would be creative and original. The paint also helped to make the surface of the cardboard waterproof.

When the project was due, the students took their boats to a lake near the school. Other students and teachers, having heard about the event and how much fun students were having building their boats, came to watch and cheer the racers on. The art teacher first graded the boats for creativity. Then he had the students put the boats in the water. Half of the cardboard boats sank before the race could even start! But that didn't upset anyone — not even the students aboard the sinking boats. They just laughed and had as much fun as the people who were watching.

The cardboard boat project was such a challenge and so much fun that the teacher decided to assign one every year. It became one of the biggest events at the school!

College students compete in a cardboard boat race.

Lots of people all over the country heard about the boat-building test and how much fun the students had. Soon, cardboard boat races started springing up in towns and cities far away from the school. Scout troops, summer camps, and company picnics all began to hold cardboard boat races. Newspapers and TV news programs began to run articles and stories about the races, telling everyone about the crazy and colorful boats and the fun that people had building and trying to race them. Cardboard boat races have become a warm-weather community event in towns and cities everywhere. And while the rules might be a little different from race to race, the goal is the same—to have a great time building and racing crazy cardboard boats!

Spectators cheer for their favorite boat.

DECISIONS, DECISIONS

So how do you get ready for a cardboard boat race? There's more to it than just gluing together a few cardboard boxes, painting them, and then crossing your fingers. Some careful planning must be done before you get out the scissors or open that bottle of glue.

Most cardboard boat builders have to make some key decisions before they begin. Do they just want to enter the race and have fun with their friends? Do they want to build a boat that truly works and actually has a chance to win the race? Or do they want to try to capture one of the prizes given for the funniest, craziest, or most creative boat?

Cardboard boats come in all shapes and sizes, including rockets, canoes, and guitars!

Most boat builders try really hard to win one of the creativity prizes. Lots of cardboard boat events give prizes for things like the prettiest boat, the funniest boat, the biggest **crew** (the greatest number of people on a boat), the best crew costumes, or the most spirited crew.

Many other racers focus their efforts on building the fastest boat. Their boats don't often look that pretty or colorful, but they are built to float well and move quickly and easily in the water.

On the other hand, the judges sometimes give an award to the boat that sinks in the funniest or most entertaining way, so racers try to build a boat that will sink on purpose!

These racers are hoping to win the best costume award.

Some boat builders try to win prizes by making their boats sink!

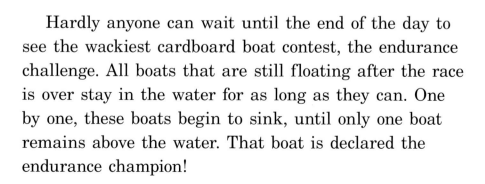

Hardly anyone can wait until the end of the day to see the wackiest cardboard boat contest, the endurance challenge. All boats that are still floating after the race is over stay in the water for as long as they can. One by one, these boats begin to sink, until only one boat remains above the water. That boat is declared the endurance champion!

SHIP SHAPE

Once racers have decided on their goals for the contest, it's time to plan the type of cardboard boat they want to build. There are almost as many different kinds of boats as there are racers to build them! Cardboard boats come in all shapes and sizes, and the different sizes and shapes work better for different purposes.

For example, a racer might build a wide, flat boat called a **raft**. A raft can have a lot of space to hold many people, and because it is flat and wide, the boat is stable and less likely to tip over. But rafts are usually slow and hard to steer. They make good boats for builders trying to win creativity or spirit prizes, but it's hard to win the race with a raft.

On the other hand, a **kayak** is long and narrow and has room for only one or two people. A kayak with a small crew doesn't win the spirit prize very often. And kayaks can tip over easier than wider boats. However, the thin shape helps a kayak slip through the water very easily. The fastest boats in most cardboard boat races are almost always different kinds of kayaks, but their crews must be good at keeping the boats from tipping over and sinking!

A really large raft can hold a big crew.

Kayaks are narrow and built for speed.

Racers also have to decide how they are going to propel their boats. The rules for some cardboard boat races allow racers to propel their boats using paddle wheels, which are big wheels with several paddles. The wheels are attached to each side of the boat and turned with bicycle pedals. But paddle wheels can be hard to build onto the boats, and sometimes they prove to be too heavy. Most builders choose to use oars to push their boats along the surface of the water. Oars are simple, they are lightweight, and they almost always work. Most cardboard boat races allow people to use oars borrowed from real boats, too.

Some boats use paddle wheels, but oars (right) are the easiest way to propel a cardboard boat.

BUILD THAT BOAT!

Some serious racers build a skeleton out of cardboard to give their boat extra strength.

So you are finally ready to start building your very own cardboard boat. Where do you get the materials? You can't just go to a hobby store and ask for a special cardboard boat kit with everything included. There is no such thing! You have to gather what you need from more than one place. You probably have some tools and materials at home, such as tape, scissors, glue, a ruler or tape measure, paper, pencils, and markers.

You might need to get paint and caulk from a paint store or building supply center. Be careful, because this stuff can be really messy. And it's always a good idea to get permission from a parent or another adult before working with materials like paint, caulk, or glue.

Corrugated cardboard can be the hardest material to find. Sometimes boat builders get their cardboard from the people holding the boat race. You could also ask grocery stores, furniture stores, or stores that sell TVs, washers, dryers, or refrigerators for any extra boxes they might let you have. Try to get the biggest, flattest pieces you can find.

MATERIALS LIST

- corrugated cardboard
- tape
- scissors
- glue
- ruler or tape measure
- drawing paper
- pencils
- markers
- paint
- caulk

Test your design by making a paper model.

You'll probably want to begin by drawing a picture of the boat you want to build. Think carefully about what your boat will look like from all sides, including the top and bottom, the left and right sides, and the front and back. As you are drawing, think about the shape of each piece of cardboard you will have to use, and try to think about what size each piece will need to be.

After you finish drawing your design, try making a small model of your boat out of paper. Putting together the model will help you think about how you will need to **assemble**, or put together, your real cardboard boat. Try floating your finished model in a tub of water. Does it move the way you want it to move? Is it stable? Does it sink like a rock?

Draw the pieces of your boat.

Cut the pieces out.

If your model doesn't seem to work, you can easily come up with another plan and try it out. That way, you haven't wasted any of your main materials on a bad design.

Once you have a model that seems to work, it's time to draw the pieces for the full-size boat onto your flat pieces of cardboard. Then cut out each piece with scissors.

When your pieces are all cut, paint both sides of each piece to make them waterproof. Then fill the edges of each piece with caulk and allow them to dry. When the caulk is dry, cover the edges with tape so water won't soak into them.

Cover both sides with paint.

Now it's time to assemble the pieces into a boat! Most builders start with the bottom of the boat, sometimes using two or three layers of cardboard to make it strong. Once you have built the bottom, glue the sides, the front, and the back of the boat onto it, and hold everything in place until all the glue dries.

HOW TO BUILD A

Once you have put your boat together, check each edge where the pieces come together for places that might not be strong enough or where water might leak into the boat. Put extra caulk in these places to seal them. Even one tiny problem spot could lead to a sinking boat!

Wait, you aren't quite finished. Most builders place their finished boats in water to test them. They look closely for any leaks or weak spots that they might have missed, and they check to see that the boat is stable. If there are leaks, let the boat dry, and then add caulk to the problem spots. If the boat isn't stable, you may have to add pieces to balance it in the water. Once you have fixed any leaks or other problems, you can decorate your boat for the big race!

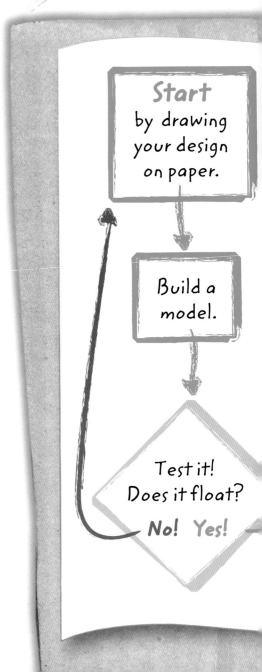

Start by drawing your design on paper.

Build a model.

Test it! Does it float?

No! Yes!

CARDBOARD BOAT

```
Build the boat          Check for
bottom and              problem
add the sides,           spots.
front, and back.
        ↑                    ↓

Cut out the             Test it!
pieces and            Does it float?
make them             No!    Yes!
waterproof.
        ↑

Draw the                Decorate
full-size             your boat!
pieces on             Great job!
cardboard.
```

THE SCIENCE OF FLOATING

Race day is nearly here, but before you take your boat down to the water to try your luck against the other builders, why not spend a little time discovering just what makes a boat—or anything else—sink or float.

All cardboard boat builders, whether they spend weeks working on their boats or just a few hours, are faced with the same basic problem—will their boats float once the crew is on board? A big boat with only one or two people aboard will float easily, but it will be hard to propel or steer. A small boat holding too many people may not float at all.

So, what makes things float, anyway? How can a huge steel ship weighing millions of pounds sail all of the world's oceans without sinking, while a stone the size of a quarter sinks straight to the bottom of a pond?

A huge tanker ship weighing millions of pounds floats easily
because of its large surface area.

People who build very large boats and ships have to understand the idea of **buoyancy,** or the science of floating. Buoyancy explains why different objects can or cannot float.

For example, imagine you are in a swimming pool. If you lie on your back and stretch out your arms and legs flat on top of the water, you will float fairly easily. But if you pull your knees to your chest and curl up into a ball, you quickly sink! What is happening?

When you are stretched out on your back, more of your body touches the surface of the pool. You are covering a larger area of the water. When you curl up, a smaller area of your body is touching the surface of the water. This idea of surface area is key to understanding buoyancy.

Water can support solid objects and hold them up.

Another important thing to understand about the science of floating is **gravity,** the force that makes things fall to the ground. While gravity pulls objects down, water tries to hold them up. The bigger the surface area of an object that the water has to push against, the easier the water can hold the object up. When the force of gravity and the force of the water are the same, the object floats.

But you have probably noticed that even objects that float will sink down into the water just a little bit. This happens because the object will push aside, or **displace,** an amount of water equal to the weight of the object.

A leaf floats on top of the water because the force of gravity and the push of the water are the same.

Try this experiment: Fill a paper cup with water and mark the level of the water on the outside of the cup with a felt marker. Then place a small block of wood into the cup. The block of wood will float, but notice that it sinks down into the water just a little. Now look at the water level on the side of the cup. See how it has come up just above the line you drew? The wooden block has displaced an amount of water equal to the weight of the block.

You don't notice the water displaced by your body in a swimming pool or by a ship in the ocean, but next time you get into a bathtub full of water, watch what happens!

wooden block

displaced water

water level without wooden block

previous water level

Placing a block of wood in a cup of water makes the water level rise. This is _displacement_.

Heavy objects with small surface areas, like rocks, displace some water but don't have much area for the water to push back against. That is why a rock will sink to the bottom of a pool or pond. When the weight of the object is more than the weight of the water it displaces, the object sinks.

This truck weighs more than the water it has displaced.

CHECK THAT OUT!

Race day has finally arrived! All the boat builders line up their finished boats on the grass beside the water. Everyone at the race—parents, racers, judges, and friends—walks back and forth admiring the clever, creative, and crazy boats. People laugh at the wacky costumes worn by some crews. Builders talk with each other about problems they faced and how they solved them. This part of the contest is almost as much fun for everybody as the race itself.

The judges award the prizes for creativity at this point, before any boats end up at the bottom of the river. It's a perfect moment to see what people can create with their wild imaginations!

Judges give high scores for creativity.

You might see a boat that looks like a sea monster, with a humped back and a long neck and tail. Over there is a steam ship, and a four-poster bed. There are pirate ships, whales, Native American canoes, a cow, and even a giant hot dog!

Other builders have tried to design and build boats that will stay afloat and win the race. The crews begin to pull on their life jackets and grab their oars. It's time to see which boats will really float!

Some boats float.

Others don't!

The racers set their boats in the water and the crews climb aboard carefully. Imagine what it would feel like to be a part of such a race! Everyone moves into place for the start, including you and your crew. Look! One or two boats have already started to sink, but their crews are smiling and laughing.

The judges ask for each crew's attention, and then they raise a red flag. At the drop of the flag, the race begins, and the crews paddle quickly but carefully with their oars. To win the race, a crew must propel its boat to the other side of the narrow river—about 75 feet, or less than the length of a basketball court. It's much harder than it looks, though, and soon one or two of the boats have pulled ahead of you and the others.

But wait! The front end of the lead boat begins to push down into the water, and soon its crew is floating and laughing and splashing in their life jackets. The other leading boat seems to be having trouble paddling in a straight line, and it starts to move in a big circle, turning away from the finish line! You and your crew watch them as you row past, and then you understand—you are in first place! All you have to do is keep moving and stay afloat! And there it is! You cross under the rope marking the finish line. You've won!

You are so proud of your winning boat that you pull it up onto the riverbank to keep it from getting any wetter. All that time and hard work were certainly worth it.

And do you know what? Cardboard boat racing is so much fun, you are already planning your boat for next year!

GLOSSARY

assemble put together from many pieces

buoyancy how easily something floats

corrugated wavy or wrinkly

crew people on a boat or ship

displace push aside

gravity force that pulls objects down
to the ground

kayak narrow, canoe-like boat

propel push or move forward

raft wide, flat boat